THE MASK OF ZORRO

Based on the screenplay by John Eskow,
Ted Elliot and Terry Rossio

LEVEL 2

Adapted by: Jane Rollason
From the Spanish adaptation by: Cecilia Bembibre
Publisher: Jacquie Bloese
Editor: Fiona Beddall
Designer: Mo Choy
Cover layout: Mo Choy
Picture research: Pupak Navabpour
Photo credits:
Page 6: C. Schaible/iStockphoto.
Pages 48 & 49: A. Muir/Zorro Productions Inc & TriStar; Everett Collection/Rex; 505 Games/Wii.
Pages 50 & 51: N. Elgar, C. Alvarez, G. Gerard/Getty Images.
Pages 52 & 53: Kean Collection, K. Wilson/Tostee.com/Getty Images; Ms Dotty/SXC; San Joaquin Valley Library.

Cover and interior images provided courtesy of Zorro Productions Inc. and TriStar Pictures Inc.

The Mask of Zorro © 2010 Zorro Productions, Inc. and © 1998 by Tristar Pictures, Inc. All Rights Reserved

Published by Scholastic Ltd. 2010
Fact Files and design © Scholastic Ltd. 2010

No part of this publication may be reproduced in whole or in part, or stored in a retrieval system, or transmitted in any form or by any means, electronic, mechanical, photocopying, recording or otherwise, without the written permission of the publisher. For information regarding permission, write to:

Mary Glasgow Magazines (Scholastic Ltd.)
Euston House
24 Eversholt Street
London NW1 1DB

Printed in Malaysia

Reprinted in 2016 and 2017

Contents

	Page
The Mask of Zorro	**4–47**
People and Places	**4**
Prologue	**6**
Chapter 1: The trap	7
Chapter 2: Behind the mask	11
Chapter 3: California's most dangerous men	16
Chapter 4: Welcome home!	20
Chapter 5: Zorro the teacher	24
Chapter 6: Zorro lives!	27
Chapter 7: Montero's party	31
Chapter 8: California gold	36
Chapter 9: Elena's story	41
Chapter 10: A fight to the end	44
Chapter 11: A new start	47
Fact Files	**48–53**
Zorro: the legend lives on!	48
The Mask of Zorro: the stars	50
California	52
Self-Study Activities	**54–56**
New Words	**inside back cover**

PEOPLE AND PLACES

DIEGO DE LA VEGA/ZORRO

is a Spanish landowner. He lives in a *hacienda* (a big house) in Spanish California with his beautiful wife, Esperanza, and their daughter. But he has another, secret life. He is Zorro, the man in black who fights for the people of California against men like Rafael Montero.

ALEJANDRO MURRIETA/ YOUNG ZORRO

is clever and strong. He has had a difficult life. His parents died when he was a boy. He has always loved Zorro, and wants to become the new Zorro.

CAPTAIN* HARRISON LOVE
is a young soldier. He has hard eyes and he doesn't smile very often. He is in love with Elena.

ELENA MONTERO
is a beautiful young woman. She lived in Spain as a child, with Rafael Montero. She believes that he is her father.

RAFAEL MONTERO
is the Spanish governor of California. He does not care about the Californian people. He cares only about himself. As a young man, he was in love with Diego de la Vega's wife, Esperanza.

TORNADO
is Zorro's black horse. He is fast, strong and frightened of nothing. He is always ready to help Zorro.

* Captain is the name for a soldier who is more important than ordinary soldiers.

PLACES

LOS ANGELES is a small *pueblo* (town) in California at the time of the story. Today it is one of the most important cities in the USA.

ZORRO'S CAVE is a secret place next to Diego de la Vega's house. Zorro trains in the cave, and he keeps Tornado here.

TALAMANTES PRISON is a terrible place. It is wet, dark and cold, and there is very little food. Living men come here, but only dead men leave.

THE GOLD MINE is secret. Only Rafael Montero and a few of his men know about it. It is in the mountains near Los Angeles.

THE MASK OF ZORRO
PROLOGUE

When this story starts, in 1821, California and Mexico have been under Spanish government for three hundred years. But that time is now ending. After many years of fighting, Mexico is a free country, and California has become part of Mexico.

General* Santa Anna now governs California from far away in Mexico. He does not have many soldiers in California, so he leaves it in the hands of the Spanish landowners. They give Santa Anna money, and the people of California are no trouble.

These changes have brought an end to Rafael Montero's fifteen years as governor of California. During that time, Montero lived like a king and took too much money from the poor. The people hated him.

Who fought for the people? Who fought against Montero? One man. He rode a black horse and wore a black mask. His name was Zorro!

* A *general* is a very important soldier.

CHAPTER 1
The trap

Rafael Montero looked down from his house onto the square below. He smiled. The square was full of people and soldiers. The people shouted up at Montero. They hated him.

He was ready to leave his job as governor of California. He planned to go to Spain. But before that there was one last thing to do. Three unlucky men stood in a line on one side of the square. Montero's soldiers stood opposite the men. Their guns were ready.

Two young brothers were watching in the square. Their names were Joaquin and Alejandro Murrieta.

'Boys,' said a voice behind them, 'this is no place for children. Go home.' It was Father Felipe. He and his church tried to help the Murrieta boys. Life was hard for them because their parents were dead.

'We are waiting for him,' said Joaquín. 'For Zorro.'

Then a man on a horse rode into the square. He stopped

outside the governor's house and ran up the stairs.

'Don* Rafael!' he called. His name was Luis Quintero. 'Santa Anna's Mexican soldiers left San Diego this morning. They will be here in a few hours. You must leave now.'

'Don Luis,' smiled Montero, 'I have a present for you before I leave.' He gave Quintero some papers. 'These papers give you land near the *pueblo* of Los Angeles.'

Quintero looked at the papers. 'This was *your* land – the Spanish governor's land,' he said.

'And I am giving it to you before Santa Anna can take it. I have given land to many of our friends in California.'

'Don Rafael, California will not be the same without you,' smiled Quintero.

Montero looked down to the soldiers in the square. 'Kill them!' he shouted.

* Important men are called *Don* in Spanish. Women are called *Doña*.

The soldiers pointed their guns at the men. One of the soldiers held up his sword. 'Ready,' he shouted. His arm came down. 'Fire!'

At the same moment, a rope went round the first gun and pulled it hard to the left. The first gun pushed the second gun to the left. Suddenly all the guns were pointing at the soldier who was giving the orders. They fired and the soldier fell. He was dead.

'Zorro!' shouted Alejandro. He and Joaquin were on top of a high building opposite.

'Zorro!' shouted someone in the square. 'Long live Zorro!'

A man in a black mask and black clothes cut the men free with his sword. He fought the other soldiers.

Montero made a sign to a soldier across the square. 'My little trap worked,' he smiled.

Alejandro and Joaquin looked down. A group of soldiers suddenly stood up below them. The soldiers pointed their guns at Zorro on the other side of the square.

'Joaquin, it's a trap!' shouted Alejandro.

There were some large pieces of wood on top of the building.

'Let's push these down,' cried Joaquin.

The boys pushed the wood off the building. It fell onto the soldiers. They dropped their guns. Everyone looked at the soldiers and Zorro disappeared into a building.

The boys waited on top of the building. Suddenly a voice behind them said, 'Thank you, my friends.'

The boys turned around quickly.

'Zorro!' said Joaquin.

Zorro took the medallion from around his neck and gave it to Joaquin. Then he jumped off the building.

'Where is he?' Montero shouted to his soldiers. He was very angry.

Suddenly he felt a sword at his neck.

'Did you want to see me before you left?' asked Zorro. There was blood on Zorro's shirt.

'You are hurt, I see,' said Montero. 'The people think you are special, but you are not. You are only a man.'

Zorro cut a 'Z' in Montero's neck with the end of his sword.

'Aaarrghh!' cried Montero.

'A present from Los Angeles,' said Zorro. 'Never come back, Montero. We do not want you here.'

The man in the mask called his beautiful black horse, Tornado, and jumped onto its back. He rode quickly out of the square.

Montero put his hand over the cut in his neck.

'You will pay for this, Zorro,' he said.

'Zor-ro! Zor-ro!' shouted the people in the square.

CHAPTER 2
Behind the mask

Zorro and Tornado rode fast out of the *pueblo*. They crossed the de la Vega lands and rode past the de la Vega home. They continued down to the beach. From there, Tornado climbed up to a large cave.

Inside the cave, Zorro jumped off Tornado and gave him food and water. 'We are getting too old for this, Tornado,' he said.

He went into a large room in the cave. There, he took off his black clothes and mask and put on a clean shirt. In the room, there were books on the tables and swords on the walls. There was also a large, empty area for training in swordfighting.

He was now Diego de la Vega, gentleman and landowner. Diego went through a secret door into his house, and then into the bedroom of his little daughter, Elena.

She was awake in her bed and looking at some flowers. Esperanza always put romania* flowers around her bed. The smell filled the room.

Diego sat beside his little girl and told her about his adventure in the town square. Elena laughed when he waved some romania flowers around like a sword.

There was someone at the door. Diego looked up. It was Esperanza.

He put his arms around his beautiful wife. They looked down at their daughter. She was asleep.

'She loves to hear your stories,' said Esperanza.

'She likes my voice, I think,' he said. 'She isn't listening to the words.'

* *Romania* flowers are big and white.

They left Elena's room.

'I was worried,' said Esperanza, and took her husband's arm. He pulled it away. 'Your arm!' said Esperanza. 'There's blood!'

'It's nothing,' said Diego. 'And you will never have to worry again. Montero is going back to Spain. The mask of Zorro will be put away. That was Zorro's last adventure.'

'What will we do?' laughed Esperanza.

'We will have a house full of children and lands full of horses. We will have parties and dances.'

'Diego,' smiled Esperanza.

'Don Diego!' shouted a voice.

They turned. There stood Rafael Montero and a group of soldiers.

'Doña Esperanza,' said Montero, 'you are as beautiful as always.'

'What brings you here, Don Rafael?' asked Diego angrily.

'I wanted to say sorry, Esperanza,' said Montero.

Esperanza did not understand.

'I am sorry that I did not win your love,' said Montero, 'and I am sorry because you are losing your husband.' He turned to his soldiers. 'Men! Hold him!'

Diego laughed. 'And what have I done?'

Montero touched Diego's arm with his sword. Blood showed through the white shirt.

'There is your answer – *Zorro*!' Montero turned again to his men. 'Take him away.'

Esperanza ran to her husband's side, but one of the soldiers stopped her. Diego quickly took a sword from the wall. He faced Montero.

The soldiers pointed their guns at Diego.

'Put your guns down. This is between us,' said Montero to his men.

The two men fought. Montero tried to cut Diego with his sword, but Diego quickly moved away. Then Montero's sword hit a light. The sword flew from his hand, and the light broke. Fire started to climb the walls. One of the soldiers fired at Diego and hit the wall behind him.

'I said no guns!' shouted Montero. He reached for his sword again.

For a moment, Diego looked at Esperanza. Montero cut Diego's side. Everyone was surprised and Montero looked pleased. But Diego moved fast, and soon he had the point of his sword at Montero's neck.

'Remember your orders, Don Rafael,' said Diego. 'This is a fight between you and me.'

'Yes,' said Montero, 'between you and all of us.'

Esperanza jumped in front of her husband. At the same moment, a soldier fired his gun at Diego. Esperanza fell to the floor, dead.

'No!' cried Diego. 'No!'

Montero went up to the soldier with the smoking gun. He put his sword through the man's body.

The house was filling with smoke. The fire was everywhere. Suddenly they heard the cry of a small child. Diego jumped up and turned to Elena's room. As he turned, Montero hit him hard on the back of the head. Diego fell to the floor.

✷ ✷ ✷

When Diego woke up, he could not move. There was rope around his hands and feet. A soldier held a gun at his head.

'Elena!' he shouted. 'Elena!'

Suddenly Montero ran from the burning house. Elena was in his arms.

'Montero!' called Diego. 'Give her to me. Let me hold her!'

Montero did not give the child to Diego. 'She has her mother's eyes, doesn't she?' he said to Diego.

'Let me go!' shouted Diego. 'You are not the governor here. When the Mexicans arrive, they will let me go. And I will follow you to the world's end.'

'I am not frightened of you, de la Vega. You are going to Talamantes Prison. Nobody will find you there.'

'Then kill me now.'

'No,' said Montero. 'I have watched you with Esperanza all these years. Now you can think about me with Elena.'

Montero turned and walked away.

Diego watched as his life disappeared.

CHAPTER 3
California's most dangerous men

The people were unhappy. It was twenty years since Montero left California, but life was no better. The Spanish landowners and their soldier friends became richer. Everyone else became poorer.

At night, in the country around Los Angeles, fathers, mothers and children disappeared from their homes. No one ever saw them again. People spoke of dark riders on horseback.

Everyone asked the same question. Where was Zorro? His people needed him but he did not come.

* * *

One hot day, three men arrived in the square of a small *pueblo*. One man was old and the other two were young. They all had long hair and dirty clothes. The old man's name was Three-Finger Jack. Jack rode a horse and pulled the others behind him with ropes around their necks.

A group of soldiers were resting in the square. They had a big box that they were taking to Los Angeles. It was full of money.

'Hey!' Jack shouted to them. 'Look who's here! I've got the Murrieta brothers.' He showed them a picture. 'Joaquin and Alejandro Murrieta,' it said under the picture, 'California's most dangerous men.' The soldiers looked at the faces in the picture and they looked at the faces of the two men.

'It's them!' they cried.

'Leave them here,' said one of the soldiers. 'We'll take them. You can collect your money from the government office in the next *pueblo*.'

'I don't think so!' shouted Jack. 'I'm not stupid.'

'How much are they offering for us?' asked Alejandro, the younger brother.

'Two hundred pesos*,' said Jack.

'Two hundred pesos each?' asked Joaquin, the older brother.

'No,' laughed Jack. 'Two hundred pesos for both of you!'

'It's not possible,' said Alejandro angrily. 'We are very dangerous men! Don't take it, Jack – it's not enough.'

A soldier hit Alejandro hard.

'Shut up!' he said.

Joaquin suddenly pulled out a gun. He pointed it at the soldier. 'Don't hit my little brother again or I'll kill you.'

'But ... you're free,' said the soldier.

'And you're stupid,' said Joaquin.

* The money in Mexico is the *peso*.

Jack and the Murrieta brothers moved quickly. They took the soldiers' guns.

'Take off your clothes,' said Jack.

'All of them?' asked the soldiers.

'All of them,' said Alejandro.

They stole the soldiers' horses and they took the box of money. Then they rode away fast.

* * *

The Murrieta brothers and Three-Finger Jack travelled for some time. Then Joaquin stopped to open the box. He used his knife.

'There!' he said. 'Hey ...'

'How much money is there?' asked Alejandro.

'It's a dead cat!' said Joaquin.

'Trouble ahead!' shouted Jack suddenly.

A line of soldiers on horses waited on the road in front of them. A man with long blond hair sat on a white horse in the centre of the line. His name was Captain Love.

The three men turned to ride back. More soldiers were on the road behind them.

'It's a trap!' shouted Joaquin.

Jack, Joaquin and Alejandro looked at each other. They jumped off their horses and started to run into the wild country. Captain Love fired his gun. Three-Finger Jack cried out and fell. The Murrieta brothers ran faster. Captain Love fired his gun again. This time Joaquin fell. Alejandro went back to his brother's side.

'No, Alejandro! Run!' said Joaquin.

'I can't leave you,' said Alejandro.

'They'll kill us both,' said Joaquin. 'Go! Now!'

Alejandro ran like the wind. Then he stopped and looked back. The soldiers stood around his brother. Love pointed his gun at Joaquin. But Joaquin quickly pulled out his own gun and fired it at himself. He was dead.

Love jumped off his horse and looked at the body. He took out his sword and angrily cut off Joaquin's head.

Much later, Alejandro came back. He saw his brother's blood, but his body wasn't there. Then Alejandro saw something else, not far away. It was his brother's medallion – Zorro's medallion. He took it and walked away.

CHAPTER 4
Welcome home!

A tall ship sat still in the water. It was near a beach not far from Los Angeles. At midnight, a small boat quietly left the ship and took a man to the beach. Someone else waited on the beach with two horses.

'Welcome home, Don Rafael,' said Captain Love.

'It is good to be back,' answered Montero. 'I enjoyed my years in Spain. But I always planned to come back here one day. And now, I want to take a last look at de la Vega.'

An hour later, the two men arrived at Talamantes Prison. A soldier was sleeping inside the door. Captain Love pushed him and he woke up.

'Señor* Montero!' he cried. 'You are back in California!'

'Let me in,' Montero ordered.

They went inside. It was a sad, dark place.

'I am looking for a man. He has been here for twenty years. His name is Diego de la Vega,' said Montero.

'People forget their names here,' said the soldier. 'Perhaps he is dead.'

The soldier took them to a long, dark room. It was wet and cold.

'Make a line,' said the soldier to the men in the room.

Montero looked at the men in the line. They were old, ill, dirty. He stopped in front of one man. Was this de la Vega?

'Which of you is Zorro?' shouted Captain Love suddenly.

No one spoke for a moment.

'I am Zorro,' said a man. 'They took my mask and sword from me ...'

* In Spanish, gentlemen are called *Señor*, married women are called *Señora* and unmarried women are called *Señorita*.

Montero looked at him carefully.

'No, I am Zorro,' shouted another man.

'I am Zorro,' said a third.

'Zorro is dead,' said Montero angrily to Love. He rode back to the beach and took the little boat back to his ship.

* * *

Something woke up inside Diego de la Vega when he saw Montero.

'I must escape,' he thought. 'I must kill Montero.'

He thought of a plan. There was a dead prisoner in the room next to his. He decided to change places with him. He pulled the dead man into his room. Then he lay on the floor of the other man's room without moving. The soldiers thought that Diego was the dead man. They threw his body into a deep hole outside the prison. Diego climbed out of the hole. He was free!

* * *

The next morning, Montero came back to the beach. This time there was a welcome party, with flowers and drinks and a lot of people.

'Don Rafael, you are welcome,' said Luis Quintero.

'Thank you, Don Luis,' said Montero.

'Thank you for the land,' said Quintero quietly in Montero's ear. 'I am now a very rich man.'

Montero smiled at him and then he turned to the people.

'I know you are not happy,' he said. 'Life is hard for you. Santa Anna and the rich landowners do nothing for you. People disappear from your *pueblos*. No one helps you – not even Zorro.'

'Zor-ro!' someone shouted.

'Where has he been for the last twenty years?' asked Montero. 'The people of California must be free. Forget Zorro. Now is the time for you to fight!'

Father Felipe was there. 'You are not on our side!' he shouted.

An old man pushed his way through the people. Montero did not see him, but it was Diego de la Vega. When he was close to Montero, he took a knife from inside his clothes. He was ready to kill Montero.

'Father!' cried a young woman.

Diego and Montero both turned to the voice. A beautiful woman of about twenty-two walked up to Diego. He nearly fell as she came near. But she walked straight past him to Montero. She took Montero's hand.

'Gentlemen,' said Montero to the landowners at the party. 'My daughter – Elena.'

A girl gave Elena some flowers.

'Thank you,' said Elena. 'What a beautiful smell!' She thought for a moment. 'I know this smell.'

'That is not possible, señorita,' said Quintero. 'They are romania flowers. They grow only in California. And this is your first visit, isn't it?'

'You are right. How strange!' said Elena.

Diego moved back. 'I cannot kill Montero now,' he thought. 'She – my beautiful Elena – believes he is her father. She loves him.' He turned and walked away.

CHAPTER 5
Zorro the teacher

Alejandro Murrieta sat in a bar in the main square in Los Angeles. He looked terrible. His hair was long and his clothes were dirty.

He finished his drink. Was it his third or his fourth?

'More,' he shouted to the barman.

'Show me your money,' said the barman.

'Money, yes,' said Alejandro. 'No. I don't have any money, but I have this.' He gave the barman a medallion.

Suddenly an old man appeared. He took the medallion.

'Hey!' said the barman.

'Leave us,' said the old man.

The barman looked into the old man's eyes. He left them.

'Where did you get this?' the old man asked Alejandro.

'It was my brother's. He died,' said Alejandro.

'I'm sorry,' the man said. 'But do you really want to buy a drink with your dead brother's medallion?'

'Maybe I'll get two drinks,' laughed Alejandro.

Suddenly, Captain Love and his men rode past the bar. Alejandro saw Love and pulled out his sword.

'That man killed my brother,' he said.

'You've had too much to drink,' said the old man. 'You can't fight.' He held Alejandro's arm.

'Enough, old man!' cried Alejandro angrily. But the old man was too strong for him.

'You want to kill that man,' said the old man. 'I can teach you to fight.'

'Why do you want to help me?' asked Alejandro.

'Because one day,' said the old man, 'long ago, you helped me.'

Alejandro looked at him carefully. 'No, it's not possible,' he said slowly. 'Zorro? I thought Zorro was dead.'

The old man looked at him.

'I *was* dead,' he said.

* * *

The old man took Alejandro to Zorro's cave. They rode past the de la Vega house.

'You are Diego de la Vega,' said Alejandro. 'I lost a brother, but you lost your wife and child. I am sorry.'

Together, they cleaned the cave.

'You will learn to fight here, Alejandro,' said Diego.

'I remember Zorro's last fight, in the square, twenty years ago!' said Alejandro.

'Yes. Rafael Montero was governor of California then. Do you remember him?'

'Of course,' answered Alejandro. 'He hated Zorro!'

'And now Montero is back. But why? We have to find out.'

'I am ready,' said Alejandro. He pulled out his sword.

'Can you use that?' asked Diego.

'Of course,' said the young man. 'This end goes into the other man.'

Diego looked at him. 'This is going to take some time.'

* * *

For many days, Diego gave Alejandro lessons in swordfighting. Alejandro had to practise again and again. He exercised and his body became stronger. He learned to move and think quickly.

Diego was pleased with his pupil. He was now a good swordfighter and he learned very quickly. But there was more.

'You want to kill Captain Love,' he told Alejandro. 'But first you will have to be friends with the landowners of California. They must believe that you are one of them. You must learn the old Spanish ways. You must learn to dance. And we will give you a haircut!'

CHAPTER 6
Zorro lives!

When Diego and Alejandro arrived in the main square, it was full of people. People were selling fruit, vegetables, drinks and clothes.

Suddenly, two soldiers came into the square with four or five wild horses.

'Look at that black one!' said Diego to Alejandro. 'What a fine horse!'

'It looks like your old horse, Tornado,' said Alejandro.

'Perhaps it is Tornado's son,' said Diego.

The soldiers were having trouble with the black horse. Suddenly it pulled away and ran through the square. People shouted and dropped the things that they were carrying. They hurried into the buildings around the square.

When the horse stopped for a moment, Alejandro ran to it. He spoke quickly in its ear. The horse stayed quietly next to Alejandro until a soldier took it away.

* * *

That night, Alejandro put on a black mask and black clothes and went back to the town square. A beautiful woman went past him. She was wearing a white dress and riding a fine white horse.

'Careful, señorita,' he said. 'There are dangerous men in this town.'

'Thank you,' said Elena to the man in the mask. 'I haven't seen any. Have you?'

Smiling to herself, she continued on her way.

* * *

Alejandro found the soldiers' rooms behind the governor's house. The soldiers were laughing and drinking. Some were cleaning their guns.

The horses were in a big room next to the soldiers. Alejandro found the black horse. 'I will call you Tornado,' he said quietly in its ear.

He climbed on its back. But when Alejandro touched the sides of the horse with his feet, the horse went wild. It jumped around the building. The soldiers heard the sound and ran in. They tried to fire their guns at Alejandro, but the horse was moving too fast. As it broke through the doors of the building, Alejandro fell off. The horse ran away.

Alejandro lay on the floor with the soldiers all around him. They had swords and they were angry. Alejandro jumped up and fought them. He hit one with his left hand, another with his right hand. He used his feet, then pulled out his sword. He remembered Diego's lessons and he fought brilliantly.

He pushed open a door into another room. In it was the soldiers' biggest gun. He fired the gun into the soldiers' room. Their beds caught fire. Everyone was shouting and running about. Alejandro escaped and ran into the church. Behind him, the room exploded and lit up the night sky.

The church was quiet. Father Felipe saw Alejandro in his black mask.

'Zorro! Is that you?' he cried.

'Yes, Father, it's me. Can you help me? The soldiers will be here in a moment,' said Alejandro.

Father Felipe opened the door to the confession box.

Alejandro sat quietly. Suddenly, he heard a woman's voice on the other side of the confession wall.

'Please hear my confession, Father,' she said.

Alejandro knew the voice. It was the woman on the white horse!

'Yes, my child,' said Alejandro.

'I try to be good, as my father wants. But I can't,' said Elena. 'I saw a man and I liked him. I can't stop thinking about him.'

'A man?'

'Yes,' said Elena. 'He was a bad man, I think. He was wearing a black mask.'

Alejandro smiled. 'This man ... was he good-looking, intelligent ...?'

'I don't know, Father. I didn't see his face,' said Elena. 'But there was something about his eyes ...'

Then Alejandro heard the soldiers. Captain Love and his men were in the church. Elena came out of the confession box.

'What are you doing here, Elena?' Captain Love asked.

'I was saying my confession,' she said.

'Who to?' asked Captain Love. 'Father Felipe is here.'

He looked at the confession box. 'Stand back!' he shouted, and fired his gun at it. Then he opened the door ... but the confession box was empty. Captain Love left the church angrily.

Alejandro found the black horse in the square and climbed on. He cut a big 'Z' in the wall and rode away into the night.

★ ★ ★

Alejandro arrived back at Zorro's cave. He was very pleased with himself.

'Look!' he shouted to Diego. 'The new Tornado! And I cut a big 'Z' in the town square. Zorro is back!'

'Zorro helps the people,' said Diego angrily. 'After all our hard work, you just want to be famous.'

'I came here to learn. I have learned to fight like Zorro. What is the problem?' said Alejandro.

'Come,' said Diego. 'No angry words tonight. We have more to learn. You will fight with this now.' He showed Alejandro a spoon. 'Montero is having a party. You must go there and find out his plans for California. But first, you must learn to be a gentleman.'

'Me? A gentleman?' laughed Alejandro. 'Now that will be a lot of work!'

'Yes,' said Diego, and he smiled.

CHAPTER 7
Montero's party

Teacher and pupil stood outside Montero's house on the night of the party. The garden was full of pretty lights and flowers.

Alejandro wore the clothes of a Spanish gentleman: a white shirt and trousers and a blue jacket. He looked rich and good-looking, but he was worried.

Diego stood behind him. 'Remember,' he said in Alejandro's ear. 'Today you are a gentleman and I work for you. My name is Bernardo.'

'Montero will know your face,' said Alejandro.

'Don't worry. I told you before. Montero never looks at his cooks, cleaners and gardeners. And he thinks I am dead. He is not looking for me so he will not see me.'

They went in. The house and garden were full of fine people in beautiful clothes. There was music and wonderful food and drink. In the garden there was a large dance floor.

Montero and Elena stood by the door and welcomed their guests.

'Good evening,' said Alejandro. 'My name is Don Alejandro del Castillo. I have just arrived from Spain. My father knows the King and Queen well.'

'Your father is Señor del Castillo?' said Montero. 'Yes, I have heard of him, but I have not met him.'

'My family has houses and lands here. I have come to see them. I am planning to buy more.'

'I am pleased to meet you,' said Montero. 'This is my daughter, Elena.'

Elena looked wonderful in a beautiful red dress. Alejandro took her hand and smiled.

'You must excuse me, señorita,' he said. 'I have not brought you an expensive present. Just this flower.' He pulled a red flower from nowhere.

'Thank you,' laughed Elena. She liked tricks like this. 'I hope you will sit at our table, señor.'

'Of course, señorita,' said Alejandro. 'You are very kind.' He turned to Diego. 'Bernardo,' he said, 'follow me.' Elena took Alejandro's arm and her father's arm.

'This is Captain Love,' said Montero to Alejandro when they reached their table. 'He is my best soldier.'

'Ah, yes, Captain Love,' said Alejandro. 'You are looking for a dangerous man, I think – a man with a mask. Have you found him?'

'Not yet,' answered Captain Love. 'But I will find him soon.'

'What do you think of Zorro, Don Alejandro?' asked Elena.

'This man Zorro,' laughed Alejandro. 'He spends

too much time on his horse and not enough time with beautiful women. He is clearly not a gentleman!'

The other men laughed.

'Zorro helps people,' said Elena.

'Perhaps, but I'm not interested in that,' said Alejandro. 'I'm interested in money.'

Elena was not talking to anyone except Alejandro, and Captain Love wasn't happy. He was in love with Elena.

He stood up. 'Elena,' he said, 'will you dance with me?'

'Thank you, Captain Love,' she said, and they walked to the dance floor.

Soon the music changed to a slow dance. Alejandro walked up to them.

'I would like to dance with Elena,' he said.

'You can see that Elena is dancing with me!' said Captain Love angrily.

'Elena is dancing,' said Alejandro. 'Her partner is trying to dance.' He took Elena's arm and they danced away.

'That man is hiding something,' said Captain Love to Quintero back at the table. 'And I am going to find out his secret.'

The music changed. It was much faster now. Alejandro took Elena's hand and looked into her eyes. She did not look away. Their dance was fast and exciting. All the other guests moved off the dance floor. Everyone watched. Montero couldn't believe his eyes! His daughter was dancing much too wildly.

When the dance was over, Montero walked up to them. He looked at Alejandro.

'I am sorry, Don Alejandro,' he said. 'My daughter does not usually dance like that. What were you thinking, Elena?'

Elena turned and walked angrily back to the table.

'Don't worry, Don Rafael,' said Alejandro. 'It is good to feel strongly about things. And Elena is a fine dancer.'

Montero smiled and invited Alejandro to a meeting with the other landowners in his study.

* * *

The men sat around a large table. Montero stood in front of them with a large map of North America. Alejandro stood at the back.

'Gentlemen,' said Montero, 'you are looking at a new, free California.'

'We are very grateful to you, Don Rafael,' said Quintero. 'We are all very rich because of you. But now you want to fight Santa Anna. Why?'

'I don't want to fight,' said Montero. He showed them some gold. 'I am going to buy California from Santa Anna, with gold. Tomorrow I will take you all to a special place. All will become clear!'

CHAPTER 8
California gold

The next day, Alejandro travelled with Montero and his friends through the dry, empty lands outside Los Angeles. They saw no people, no homes.

Finally they came to a mine. Alejandro looked at the men, women and children working at the mine. They were thin and tired. And Alejandro knew some of their faces. They were people who disappeared from their homes a few years ago.

The mine went into the side of a mountain. Montero took his friends down to a cave at the bottom of the mountain. It was full of shining pieces of gold.

'This is Santa Anna's land,' said Montero. 'But he doesn't know that there is gold here. I am going to tell him that this gold is Spanish. Look – we have put the sign of the Spanish King and Queen on it. We will pay Santa Anna with his own gold, and California will be ours!'

Suddenly, there was a loud explosion.

'What was that?' Alejandro asked Captain Love.

'We get the gold out of the mountain that way,' said Captain Love.

'And where do all these workers come from?' he asked.

'We find them everywhere,' laughed Captain Love. His face was hard and cold.

From the mouth of the mine, an old man shouted, 'Welcome to this horrible place, gentlemen!'

Alejandro knew that voice. It was Three-Finger Jack! Suddenly, Jack laughed – a loud, mad laugh – and pointed at Captain Love. 'You shot me and brought me here. Why? Because I took food and horses. But you – you take people's lives!'

Captain Love was angry. He took out his gun and fired it at Jack in front of everybody. Jack fell down dead.

Montero and his friends laughed and walked away. Alejandro went to Jack and looked at him sadly for a moment. He wanted to kill Love right there. But he did nothing. The time was not yet right. He must play the part of a gentleman.

Captain Love was watching Alejandro. 'He knew that man!' he thought. Suddenly he understood. 'So that's his secret! Don Alejandro is Alejandro Murrieta.'

When everyone arrived back at Montero's house, Captain Love invited Alejandro to his office.

'A drink, Don Alejandro?' he said.

'Thank you, no,' said Alejandro. 'I have to get back to my house.'

'Well, I will have a drink,' said Captain Love. He put a large glass jar on the table. Inside was a man's head –

Joaquin's head. Love took a drink from the jar. He watched Alejandro's face very carefully as he drank. Alejandro looked hard into the eyes of his brother's killer.

After a moment he asked, 'Who is this unlucky man?'

'His name was Joaquin Murrieta. He had a brother with long wild hair. Perhaps you have seen him?'

'I have seen many men with long wild hair, Captain.'

'I have another jar like this one. It is waiting for the other brother. In fact, his name was Alejandro. How strange ... .'

'I hope you find him, Captain,' said Alejandro. He took a small glass and filled it from the jar. He drank it and left the office.

* * *

Later, Montero and Captain Love were discussing their plans in Montero's study. Quintero arrived with some news.

'Santa Anna has agreed to the plan. He will sell California to us. We are going to meet in a little *pueblo* eight kilometres from Los Angeles. We will give him the gold there,' said Quintero.

'That is fantastic news, Don Luis. We must have a drink.' Montero got some glasses. 'To a new California!'

A soldier ran into the room. 'Don Rafael!' he shouted. 'Look out of the window!'

They all ran to the window. They saw a fire on the hillside opposite. A 'Z' of fire.

'Zorro did this,' said Montero. 'He knows about the mine. Santa Anna must not find out, or we are dead.'

'The mine must disappear,' said Captain Love. 'The mine, the workers, everything. What about a big explosion? Then no one will know that the mine was ever there.'

Zorro listened to the men. He was hiding behind a cupboard in the room. When Montero and Quintero went out, Zorro quietly moved to the table. He took the map of the mine and put it inside his jacket. Then he took out his sword and jumped in front of Captain Love.

They fought. They were both brilliant swordfighters, but Zorro was better. Montero came back and joined the fight. Zorro did not stop. He fought the two men all over the house and into the garden. More soldiers joined in with their swords, but Zorro was faster than all of them. He escaped over a wall.

He watched the soldiers as they looked for him. Then he went back through the building. He was leaving through the back door when he heard a voice.

'What are you taking from my father's house?' Elena shouted. She was wearing her night clothes.

'Nothing!' cried Zorro.

'I don't believe you,' said Elena, and she held up her sword. 'I had my first swordfighting lesson when I was four. So take care.'

Zorro smiled and took out his sword. They fought.

'You're not bad,' said Elena, and she smiled.

'You're not bad either,' said Zorro. He moved quickly and cut her nightdress with his sword. Their bodies were very close. He looked into her eyes and she smiled.

It was not a fight. It was a game. A dance. Zorro cut her nightdress again and again, until it fell to the floor. Elena cried in surprise. Now she wore only some thin trousers. Her face went red.

'Excuse me,' said Zorro. He smiled and left.

Montero appeared with his men. 'What has happened? Did you see him?' he asked.

'Yes,' said Elena. 'I fought him, but he was too strong.'

Montero and his men ran outside. They jumped onto their horses and rode after Zorro.

Elena watched them. She smiled to herself.

CHAPTER 9
Elena's story

Zorro escaped from Montero and his men and reached the cave. Diego was waiting.

Alejandro showed him the map. He told him his plan to save the workers at the mine.

'I'm sorry, Alejandro. You must go alone,' said Diego.

'What? Why?'

'I have something else to do. I have to save my daughter,' he said.

'Your daughter?' said Alejandro. 'Of course ... Elena! Montero didn't kill your daughter. He took her to Spain.'

'Yes,' said Diego. 'I know that you love her. I love her too. Elena is the most important thing for me now.'

'What about California? And the people?' asked Alejandro.

'They have Zorro,' said Diego. 'I have taught you everything that I know. You are ready.'

* * *

Captain Love arrived at Montero's house and went to the study. Montero was looking at the map of the new California.

'Did you find him?' asked Montero.

'No, but I *will*,' said Captain Love.

Suddenly, Diego was in the room. He put his sword at Montero's neck.

'Call Elena,' he said quietly to Montero.

Montero went white. He was frightened of the look on de la Vega's face. What was he planning to do? Montero loved Elena. He didn't want to lose her now.

He sent Love to find Elena. She came quickly.

'What's happening, Father?' she shouted. 'This is Bernardo, Don Alejandro's man. Why does he have a sword at your neck?'

'This man does not work for Don Alejandro. He is Diego de la Vega,' said Montero. 'He says that he is your father. But he is an old man. He is not right in the head.' He smiled.

'De la Vega,' said Elena. 'I remember that name.'

'I am your father, Elena. I put flowers on your bed when you were a baby,' he said with a soft voice. 'I told you stories before you fell asleep.'

'The flowers ... I remembered the smell of the flowers of California,' said Elena. 'And your voice ... I can hear it in my past.'

'Put down your sword, Don Diego,' said Montero, 'or my soldiers will kill you ... in front of my daughter!'

Diego looked at Elena. She was crying. He put down his sword and went with Montero's soldiers.

'She knows,' he said to Montero. 'She knows.'

* * *

Later, Elena left her room very quietly. She looked and listened. There was nobody around. Quickly, she went down the stairs. She found Diego and unlocked his door.

'You are my father,' she said. 'I saw a real father's love for his daughter in your face this evening. I have never seen that in Montero's face.'

'You are so like your mother, Elena. She was beautiful and clever and strong, like you.'

'I hope I am a little like you too, Father. I hope I am like Zorro, the people's fighter!'

'Perhaps you are better than Zorro. I have heard that you are a brilliant swordfighter.'

Elena took her father's hand.

'Tell me about our life together – before Montero,' she said. 'I want to know everything.'

They sat together, and Diego told her the story of her life.

CHAPTER 10
A fight to the end

Zorro put on some long brown clothes and walked through the mine. The workers did not look at him. They were tired and ill. They thought that he worked there.

Captain Love arrived. 'Get the workers down into the mine and lock the doors!' he shouted to his men.

Zorro watched as Love's men pushed the workers behind the doors. 'Tomorrow there will be nothing here,' laughed one of the soldiers.

The gold was in a big box outside the mine. Montero was waiting for it at the top of the mountain. The men put the box onto a lift and Captain Love climbed up next to the gold. 'Pull!' he shouted to the men at the top of the mountain. 'Start the fire,' he shouted to the men outside the mine.

The box was halfway up the mountain when suddenly it stopped. Love looked up. Zorro! Now he was in his black clothes and mask and he was fighting with the men at the top.

Montero saw Zorro too, and pulled out his gun. But before he could fire at him, he felt a sword in his back. It was Diego ... with Elena.

The two old men fought. Diego hit Montero's arm and he dropped his sword.

'Now I can kill you,' said Diego.

'No,' said Elena. She ran between the two men – her two fathers.

Montero put his arm around Elena, then put his gun to her head.

'Drop the sword,' he said to Diego.

Diego dropped his sword. Montero fired his gun and Diego fell. There was blood on his shirt. Elena wanted to help him. But the workers in the mine were shouting for help too. There was fire all around them. They could not escape.

'Open the doors!' Diego shouted to Elena. Elena climbed down towards the mine. She had a gun and fired it at the lock. Zorro helped her. The lock broke and the people ran out. They were just in time. Seconds later, the doors caught fire and smoke filled the entrance to the mine.

Zorro climbed up onto the lift. He started fighting with Captain Love.

'I will kill you as I killed your brother,' shouted Love.

As they fought, the lift went down suddenly. Love couldn't stay on his feet. He fell ... onto Zorro's sword.

At the top of the mountain, Montero heard Love's cries. He looked down. He saw Zorro jumping off the lift, just in time. Love and the gold were falling and falling.

Suddenly there was a great explosion. It threw Montero into the air. The side of the mountain fell on top of Captain Love and all the gold. Love and Montero were dead.

Zorro took off his mask and ran to Diego. He was lying in Elena's arms.

'You're Zorro now,' Diego said to Alejandro. 'Your people need you.'

Diego looked at his daughter. 'You are so beautiful, like your mother. I have found you, and now I am losing you again.'

Elena started to cry. Diego took her hands and Alejandro's hands, and put them together. And then he died.

CHAPTER 11
A new start

Alejandro was telling his little son a bedtime story. It was about Zorro and his last adventure. There were flowers around the little boy's bed.

'When Zorro died, everyone came to say goodbye,' said Alejandro. 'We will never forget your grandfather, little Joaquin. But now a new Zorro fights for the people!' Alejandro started to dance around the room. He waved some flowers like a sword. The little boy smiled. 'To fight for good with his sword ...'

Elena came into the room. She looked at her husband. He stopped waving the flowers.

'To fight ... very carefully,' he said.

Elena put her arms around Alejandro.

'Where can I find this Zorro?' she asked him.

'You know Zorro,' he smiled. 'He could be anywhere.'

THE END

FACT FILE

ZORRO:

For almost 100 years, Zorro has been one of the world's most popular heroes. He's a brilliant horserider and a fantastic swordfighter. He wasn't a real person, but you can follow his adventures in books, in films, on TV and in the theatre. And now you too can be Zorro in a new video game.

THE BOOKS

Johnston McCulley created Zorro in 1919 in a book called *The Curse of Capistrano*. *Zorro* means *fox* in Spanish. People loved the book and they loved Zorro. McCulley wrote more than sixty adventures about his hero.

How did Diego de la Vega become Zorro? In 2005 Isabel Allende, a famous writer from Chile, answered this question in her story, *Zorro*, about Diego's life as a boy and a young man.

THE FILMS

Zorro first appeared in cinemas in 1920. The actor Douglas Fairbanks played Zorro. Thousands of people went to cinemas to watch the man in the black mask. Since then, Zorro has been the hero of more than fifty films and TV shows. *The Mask of Zorro* is one of the most famous films. A second film starring Antonio Banderas and Catherine Zeta-Jones came out in 2005. It is called *The Legend of Zorro*. And there are plans for a third Zorro film.

the legend lives on!

THE MUSICAL
In the musical story of his life, Zorro dances and sings to the fast guitar music of The Gypsy Kings. *Zorro: the Musical* opened in London in 2008. It will soon be in theatres in Europe, South America and the Far East.

AND THEN ... THE VIDEO GAME
In 2009, Zorro came to life in a new video game for the Nintendo Wii and the Nintendo DS. In *The Destiny of Zorro*, players become Zorro as he fights for the people of California. Now everyone can be a hero with a sword!

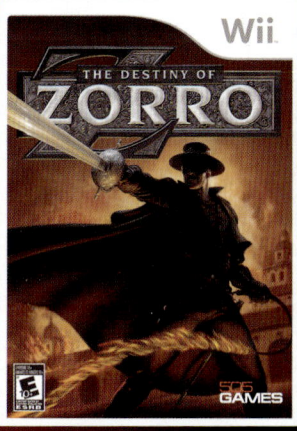

> Diego de la Vega is a rich and quiet man. Zorro is brave and mysterious. Do you know any other heroes with two different sides? What are they like?

What do these words mean? You can use a dictionary.

legend   hero   mysterious   to create   musical   brave

FACT FILE

THE MASK OF ZORRO:

Antonio Banderas

Catherine Zeta-Jones

Anthony Hopkins

Can you swordfight in a mask? Can you ride a horse fast across the countryside? Can you speak English with a Spanish accent? The stars of *The Mask of Zorro* had to learn all these skills before they started making the film!

Antonio Banderas (Alejandro)

❝Zorro has to fight with a sword while he is wearing a mask. I couldn't see very well. It was really hard!❞

Before filming, the Spanish actor practised swordfighting for two months with the best teachers in Europe.

Antonio was already a good horserider, but he had to do some difficult things on horseback in the film. He practised very hard.

❝The horse knew when we were filming. When the director shouted "Go!" the horse lifted his head for the cameras.❞

the stars

Catherine Zeta-Jones (Elena)

Catherine Zeta-Jones is a British actress. She was born in Wales. For the film, she learned to speak English with a strong Spanish accent. She also learned swordfighting.

❝The fight scene between Elena and Zorro is like a dance. It's our love scene. It wasn't easy to do a scene without most of my clothes! I didn't feel comfortable, but luckily my hair is very long!❞

Catherine is a great dancer. You can see her dancing in the films *Chicago* and *Death Defying Acts*. In *The Mask of Zorro*, she had to learn some Spanish-American dances for the scene between Elena and Alejandro at Montero's party.

❝I practised the dance in Mexico. It was great fun!❞

Anthony Hopkins (Diego)

❝I love Zorro. He is elegant but he is funny too.❞

Anthony is a British actor and, like Catherine Zeta-Jones, he comes from Wales.

Anthony had to work hard to be ready for the film. He exercised every day and did a lot of horse riding. He also learned to use a whip. The film makers wrote a scene in Zorro's cave just to show Diego's skill with his whip!

> Which would you most like to learn: swordfighting, Spanish dancing or horse riding? Why?

> What do these words mean? You can use a dictionary.
> **skill   actor/actress   director   accent   scene   elegant   whip**

FACT FILE

CALIFORNIA

Today California is one of the biggest and most important states in the USA. But what was life like for the early Californians?

THE FIRST EUROPEANS

Christopher Columbus travelled from Spain to America in 1492, and many people soon followed him across the Atlantic Ocean. At first, most of them were Spanish soldiers. Two soldiers called Francisco de Ulloa and Juan Rodríguez Cabrillo discovered California and claimed it for Spain. California was in two parts at that time: Alta California (today, the state of California in the United States) and Baja California (today, part of Mexico).

THE MISSIONS

The Spanish Kings and Queens wanted their new lands in America to be Catholic. Between 1600 and 1800, they sent Catholic priests there to build missions. The priests lived in the missions and started schools there. American Indians lived with them and learned to be Catholic. The priests brought new music, plants and animals to California, and Spanish ways of growing food. The lives of these Indians changed forever.

GOLD!

In 1848, after some fighting between Mexico and the United States, Alta California became part of the United States. But the same year, California became famous for something else. A man called James Marshall discovered gold! In 1849, more than 300,000 people arrived in California from other parts of the United States and abroad. They were called the 'Forty-Niners' and they all wanted to find gold. A few became very rich, but most of them made no money from gold.

BANDITS!

Joaquín Murrieta

California was now a dangerous place. Looking for gold was hard and people were very poor. Miners from outside California had to pay the government to work there. Some became bandits. People told stories about a famous bandit called Joaquin Murrieta. Murrieta travelled around California and took other people's money and horses. We can't be sure that he was real. But many people believe that Murrieta was like England's Robin Hood – he took from rich people and gave to poor people.

CALIFORNIA TODAY

California is famous for its beaches and surfing, and of course for its films. Hollywood is in California's biggest city, Los Angeles.

In 1849, many people from outside California went to work in the California gold mines. Are there many people from abroad in your country? What work do they do?

What do these words mean? You can use a dictionary.
bandit   to claim   state   mission   priest   plant

SELF-STUDY ACTIVITIES

Prologue–Chapter 2

Before you read

Use your dictionary for these questions.

1 Match the words and meanings.

cave cut flower gold mask medallion mine neck prison rope square sword trap

- a) When you wear this, people can't see your face.
- b) This is very expensive and shines brilliantly in sunlight.
- c) You can climb mountains safely if you use this.
- d) This is a big open place in the centre of a town.
- e) You use this to catch an animal.
- f) Before people built houses, they lived in this.
- g) This joins your head to your body.
- h) You wear this around your neck. It is sometimes gold.
- i) This grows in gardens. It smells nice and looks pretty.
- j) A knife can give you this. It hurts!
- k) If a person kills someone, they usually go to this place.
- l) In the past, people often used this in a fight.
- m) This is a deep hole in the ground where people work.

2 Who's who? Put the right people in the sentences.

soldier gentleman governor

- a) The most important person in California is the ... .
- b) A ... often has to fight in other countries.
- c) A ... comes from a good family. He always knows the right words to say.

3 Look at 'People and Places' on pages 4–5.

- a) Who is married to Esperanza?
- b) Who was very young when his parents died?
- c) Who lived in Spain when she was young?
- d) Who is the governor of California?
- e) Who is in love with Elena?
- f) What is the name of Zorro's horse?
- g) What secret place does Zorro have?
- h) What secret place does Montero have?

After you read

4 Choose the correct words.
   a) **Mexico** / **Spain** now governs California.
   b) The Murrieta boys want to see **Father Felipe** / **Zorro**.
   c) The soldiers kill **the three men** / **another soldier**.
   d) Zorro lives in **a cave** / **a large house**.
   e) Montero is **happy** / **angry** when his soldier kills Esperanza.
   f) **Diego** / **Montero** saves Elena from the fire.

5 What do you think? What will happen to these people?
   a) Diego   b) Elena   c) Montero

Chapters 3–6

Before you read

6 Put these words in the right sentences.
   confession   explode   wild
   a) If you don't brush your hair for a week, it looks … .
   b) If you want to make a …, you go to church.
   c) If a car catches fire, it can sometimes … .

7 The next chapter is 'California's most dangerous men'. Who are these dangerous men, do you think?

After you read

8 Answer the questions.
   a) What's inside the box?
   b) Who kills Joaquin?
   c) What does Alejandro find after the soldiers leave?
   d) Why do the soldiers throw Diego into a hole?
   e) When Elena cries 'Father!', who is she talking to?

9 True or false? Correct the false sentences.
   a) Alejandro is drinking too much in the bar.
   b) He is already a good swordfighter when he meets Diego.
   c) Diego remembers Alejandro's face.
   d) Alejandro exercises hard in Zorro's cave.

SELF-STUDY ACTIVITIES

   e) Alejandro goes to the *pueblo* to see Elena.
   f) Elena talks to Father Felipe in the confession box.

10 What will happen between Elena and Alejandro, do you think?

Chapters 7–11

Before you read

11 Do you have any **jars** at home? What do you keep in them?

12 Look at the pictures on pages 32 and 34. Will Montero and his friends believe that Alejandro is a gentleman, do you think?

After you read

13 Who is speaking? Who to?
   a) 'I work for you. My name is Bernardo.'
   b) 'My father knows the King and Queen well.'
   c) 'Zorro helps people.'
   d) 'You can see that Elena is dancing with me!'
   e) 'I am sorry. My daughter does not usually dance like that.'
   f) 'I am going to buy California from Santa Anna, with gold!'

14 Answer the questions.
   a) Who are the workers at the mine?
   b) Who does Captain Love kill in front of everybody?
   c) Whose head does Captain Love keep in a jar?
   d) Why do Montero and Captain Love change their plans when they see the 'Z' of fire?
   e) Why isn't Elena angry when Zorro escapes?
   f) Why does Elena believe Diego's story, and not Montero's?

15 What happens to these people at the end of the story?
   a) the workers in the mine
   b) Montero and Love
   c) Diego de la Vega
   d) Elena and Alejandro

16 Is Alejandro a good Zorro, do you think? In what ways is he a different Zorro from Diego de la Vega?